TEXAS
on my mind

FALCON®

Design, typesetting, and other prepress work
by Falcon, Helena, Montana.
Printed in Korea.

Library of Congress Number: 89-080766
ISBN 0-937959-69-3

FALCON®

Front cover photos

DAVID MUNECH *bluebonnets and paintbrush in the Hill Country*
WILLIAM D. ADAMS *Texas state flag*

Back cover photos

D.K. LANGFORD/NATURAL SELECTION *herding longhorns*
LARRY MAYER *Padre Island*
ENTHEOS *prairie dogs*

For extra copies of this book

Write to Falcon, P.O. Box 1718, Helena, MT 59624,
or call toll-free 1-800-582-2665

AMERICA
on my mind
series

Sunrise from Galveston Island   DAVID MUENCH

introduction

It is hard to write an introduction to Texas for several reasons. The first is size. Texas is just so big that what you might say about one part of the state simply won't do for another part. Alaska is larger, you say . . . yes, but Alaska, while containing some of the world's most spectacular scenery, lets one section fold into another with a progressive change so that its extremes aren't as unexpected.

The second difficulty in presenting Texas is its *diverse* peoples. For example, what language should you use describing Texans? English, to be sure, and Spanish, which truly is a second language for the Lone Star State. But you will still find German-speaking Texans in their third and fourth generations, you may find a French language inheritance in scattered parts of Texas, and the various East Asians, Vietnamese, Cambodians, and Laotians are creating an audible new presence in many areas of the state.

This, in turn, leads to a third difficulty for the writer: short of launching an encyclopedia, how can you do justice to all these diverse Texans? The so-called Anglo population may hold numerical superiority in Texas, but the black and Hispanic citizenry is widespread and numerous. The various ethnic contributions to Texas history and Texas culture have given the state a great array of colorful, mythical, and historical characters and ideas. The Texas cowboy, for instance, was a direct descendent of the Mexican *vaquero*. Most of the cowboy's equipment, and ranching terms, from *bronco* and *buckeroo* to *lasso* and *lariat*, arrived via Mexican Texans. And what would Texas musical history be without the great black singers of past and present, names like Leadbelly, Blind Lemon Jefferson, Lightnin' Hopkins, and Mance Lipscomb? And the worldwide vocabulary of the petroleum business developed mostly in Texas, as did many of the internationally famous oil companies.

But the final difficulty a writer writing about Texas encounters has less to do with such tangibles as landscape, language, or racial multiplicity, although they contribute to it. No, the final difficulty for the writer-about-Texas is the powerful Texas image. There are only half a dozen or so states that, on hearing their name, instant images spring to mind, and of those the Texas image is probably the strongest. One person sees a rolling prairie with cowboys on horseback, another imagines a fast-paced city like Houston, or famous athletes, coaches, and teams. Some picture historic spots like the Alamo, and nearly everyone carries a notion of

strong, handsome men and independent, beautiful women in their Texas inventory. Texas characters are thought to be bigger than life. What would Texas be without the pervasive image of the wildcatter and wheeler-dealer?

Why should this mythic identity pose a difficulty? Well, write about a Texas that does *not* fit the mythic picture, or fits it in ways unsuitable to common perception, and you run the risk of being held a Lone Star chauvinist or a Texas-style fabricator (which is a plain ol' liar raised to the *n*th power). Try to say that only a relatively tiny part of the state is sandy or desert, or try to explain that the tall, manlike *saguaro* cactus is found no closer than five hundred miles to Texas, that not one barrel of oil has been struck in Dallas County, that when a Texan says *"Y'all"* it always indicates more than one person, that not all Texas men top six feet and not all women place in the Miss America contest (although it's been won by a number of Texans), or that most Texans don't drive a pickup truck or own a pair of cowboy boots or a ten-gallon hat . . . not to mention a ranch, a saddle horse, or a Colt .45—and see how far you get!

On the other hand, it is just as difficult to convince most people that the majority of Texas' population is urban, not rural, living in

State Fair in Dallas   RICHARD REYNOLDS/TEXAS DEPT. OF COMMERCE

cities, not on farms and ranches; that Texas' manufacturing is bigger than its agriculture; that almost one-third of Texas is covered by forests; that Texas has mountains higher than any east of the Mississippi River. There are many places in Texas that are cool in the summer, especially after the sun goes down—although that Texas sun is no myth!—and a corner of Texas somewhat larger than most New England states is annually among the wettest spots in the United States.

What is Texas, then? It is a place united in the minds of its people by history, heroes, and heroines, by legend and popular image. Long before movies and television, Texans were, consciously or unconsciously, forming the Texas mystique, the perception of a place where opportunity abounds, where wealth and happiness are there for the taking, where everyone greets you with a smile and a big "Howdy," where there's freedom to be, well, *eccentric,* where you know all your neighbors (who'll pitch in and help when bad luck hits you), and where a handshake or an "Okay" can seal a million-dollar deal.

Still, despite going under one name and sharing one image, Texas is actually several different places. I refer to them as the five states of Texas. Each has recognizable characteristics of geography, geology, and demography to distinguish it from its neighbors. And here's a historical note: by virtue of its annexation treaty with the United States, Texas

has the power to divide itself into as many as five separate states if it should so choose. (But it won't happen, J. Frank Dobie, the Texas folklorist and author predicted, because who'd get the Alamo?)

My five states of Texas generally follow the compass north, south, east, and west—although subdivisions within each are recognized by Texans. First, I would list West Texas because West Texas is easily bounded and its inhabitants easily brought to mind. West Texas begins on the western shore of the Brazos River and extends a few hundred miles almost to (but not including) El Paso. (Though farther west than West Texas, El Paso is *El Paso*...a country of its own.)

West Texas is so huge it is often broken into "Central West Texas," or the "Trans-Pecos" region, or "under the Caprock," or the "Panhandle," the "High Plains," or the "Llano Estacado." It calls itself "The Big Country": big ranches, big space, big sky, big spirited people. Further designation is seldom needed when you remark, "He (or she) is a West Texan." If there is a legendary Texas figure, this is it: tough, but always says "Ma'am," gambles on life, the weather, and cards, drives too fast, is stoutly loyal. West Texas women never say, "Sir," and throughout history, have been famed for their ability to take over and run things, often better than their men.

East Texas is the second most easily recognized "state" of Texas. It stretches from the Red River on the north almost to the Gulf of Mexico on the south, and from the Louisiana and Arkansas borders on the east to near Dallas on the west. But it does not include Dallas, even though Big D is within a frog-hop of East Texas.

East Texans are held to be canny traders and down-home philosophers, something on the order of a Maine down-easter, perhaps, the slick-hick who can hold his own with the city-slicker. Texas tradition has it that most of the big-city used car salesmen are from East Texas. With its older history and its antebellum background, East Texas is more Southern than any other part of Texas, but don't look for "Gone With the Wind" plantation mansions or rich relics of the Lost Cause. East Texas wasn't that Southern—or that rich.

South Texas is a region that begins below a line running through Victoria, San Antonio, and Laredo on the north, dropping all the way to the tip of Texas at Brownsville. It includes the Gulf coastal area from Corpus Christi northward, and all of Padre Island. In the interior of south Texas one finds the country originally called "The Wild Horse Desert" because, despite barren topography, the land supplied enough grass and water to support huge herds of wild

The road to Alpine WILLIAM D. ADAMS

horses and wild longhorns in the 19th century, forming the cradle of the cattle industry.

To the rest of Texas, South Texas is almost a foreign country, especially along the Rio Grande border with Mexico, where citizens of both nations cross in huge numbers daily. Spanish is heard more often than English in such South Texas towns as San Diego, San Ygnacio, Rio Grande City, Zapata, or Crystal City.

South Texas is the home of "The Magic Valley," a semi-tropical section which supplies a lot of America's fruits and vegetables. Part of Matagorda Island, on the Gulf Coast, is a bird sanctuary that is home of the nation's most famous endangered species, the whooping crane. South Texas is a land of contrasts— contrasts in landscapes, people, and customs. Along the coastal and river edges it is exciting and inviting; in the interior, the country can be mysterious and, for some visitors, romantic.

If West Texas, East Texas, and South Texas are universally recognized as provinces within the state, does that mean that North Texas and Central Texas are as easily identified? No, it does not. Although the designation "North Texas" is applied to a specific territory, and "Central Texas" covers a large area, neither carries the impact on the public imagination of the above-noted sections. Say to a Texan that someone is a North Texan and you might get a puzzled, certainly an uncertain, look. Although North Texas includes the northeastern corner of Texas, and goes west along the Red River to Wichita Falls and southward almost to Waco, it's not nearly the defining term of those first three "states."

North Texas is, other than geographical, the legendary home of the merchant class, a region often accused of holding itself a little above, thinking itself just a little better than the rest of the state. Some observers say this comes from Dallas being its "capital." There is a lot of good-natured name-calling between Dallas and the rest of the state, much as between Los Angeles and the rest of California. "Big D" is not always applied in admiration by other Texas cities. Yet despite its location and importance to the area, Dallas seldom thinks of itself as a North Texas city, and Fort Worth, only twenty-nine miles west, almost never does. For years Fort Worth called itself, "Where the West Begins" because of its huge cattle and livestock industry, but that declined in the 1960s and the Fort Worth Stockyards, famed for cowboy, rancher, and farmer customers, is now a historic district and an entertainment center.

Along the Red River Valley, however, is a slower-paced, more rural North Texas, with lots of grain fields and vegetable patches. King Cotton, the agricultural monarch that seventy years ago ruled North Texas and made Dallas one of the largest cotton markets in the world, has moved his throne to the lower Rio Grande Valley and the irrigated farms of the High Plains. Today not a cotton gin can be found in Dallas or surrounding counties.

Central Texas, as one might suppose, centers around Austin, the state capital. Although use of the designation as cultural or social indicator has declined in recent years, "Central Texas" still represents not only a geography but a mindset. Central Texas is where so many Texas politicians come from, way out of proportion to any other part of the state. President Lyndon B. Johnson was the characteristic Texas politician, and he was from Central Texas—actually, a part of Central Texas called the Hill Country. Vice President John Nance Garner spent his adult years in Central Texas. Texas' only woman governor, Miriam A. "Ma" Ferguson, was from Central Texas, as was her husband, the governor before her, and more Central Texans have been governors, senators, or representatives, in both the state house and the national capital, than from the rest of Texas combined. An area that touches each of the other areas must breed sons and daughters who have learned compromise, balance, and getting along: foundation stones for successful political careers.

I mentioned the Hill Country. This is the region most Texans consider the state's prime vacation and hunting ground. It lies west and northwest of Austin and north of San Antonio and contains rugged hills and canyons, running streams, springs, vistas, and other pleasant items

A young cowboy MATT BRADLEY

not always found in many parts of Texas. Lots of vacation homes are in the Hill Country, and despite the fact that this is not traditional Big Ranch country, the major Texas dude ranches (yep, Texas has dude ranches!) are located here. Also, that German speaking section mentioned earlier is centered around Fredericksburg, in the Hill Country, and Fredericksburg itself is a kind of outdoor museum of the 19th century with many of its quaint houses restored by families from San Antonio, Houston, and Dallas.

What about Houston, Dallas, San Antonio? Although they're located in specific parts of Texas, they're their own "states." Only San Antonio might be classified as unique, due to its Hispanic history and culture and its role in Texas history—the Alamo, of course, is located in San Antonio, along with several 18th century Spanish missions. Houston's major difference from Dallas and San Antonio is its port, one of the busiest in the United States, and Houston seems to attract more European residents, but otherwise, Houston and Dallas share most of the attractions, and some disadvantages, of all major cities.

If I am accused of overlooking the beauty of Texas, the natural attractions and impressive sights and scenes, forgive this native son. No part of Texas is featureless, not even the rolling High Plains, or the level Panhandle. But in Texas, beauty must often be sought to be found. There is plenty of natural beauty—the beauty of the wind feeling its way along grassy ridges, acres of wildflowers climbing the hillsides, the beauty of limitless space where one welcomes the feeling of aloneness, of being close to the beginning of things. And stark beauty is found in all the vast Trans-Pecos region, the Guadalupe Mountains, the history-soaked Davis Mountains, the cloud-floating Chisos Mountains of Big Bend National Park.

There is the dark beauty of the ghostly waterways of Caddo Lake in East Texas (largest natural lake in Texas), and the sheer wildness of that region's famed bird-haunted Big Thicket. The Hill Country is more than satisfactory to

the eye that seeks quietly dramatic surroundings, and the first impulse of visitors is usually, "I'd like to retire here!" The Texas Gulf Coast stretches for hundreds of inviting miles from Galveston downward, drawing thousands of "snowbirds" from the chilly north each winter—Galveston itself being a fascinating city, retaining its wealthy 19th century aura.

But the Texas that is known or imagined the world over is not just a natural phenomenon. Texas has been created—out of passionate feelings, and bold deeds, and brave people, not only from the past but of the present. That is why, in trying to introduce the state piece by piece, I have put so much emphasis on differences and diversity. One cannot just say, "See the mountains," or "Don't miss the seashore." One cannot suggest merely visiting Dallas, or Houston, or Fredericksburg, or San Antonio; they are not "Texas," even though they are a big part of the Texas image.

In Gulf ports you can find shrimpers and fishermen as salty as any in New England. Fur hunters and trappers still make a living in some woodsy corners of the state. Roughnecks and tool-pushers labor on the petroleum drilling rigs, while Texas highways pass thousands of pump jacks for Texas oil. You can still find real cowboys in West Texas, herding cattle on horseback as well as in a jeep or by helicopter. But that's not "Texas," either.

Texas is the only state that was once an independent nation. Texas, unique among American states, owns its public lands; if the federal government wants to create preserves or forests it has to buy the land or get it as a gift. These factors have played a definite part in creating the imaginary Texans, bigger than life, heroic men and beautiful women of all races. Texas loves winners, whether it be in football or beauty contests. But with all its emphasis on winning, on success, on bigness and boldness (the state song, "Texas, Our Texas," speaks of "...boldest and grandest...."), it is a place with a heart. There is a quaint admonition still seen along many Texas highways, "Drive Friendly." The grammar may be questionable, but the sentiment is genuine. Seldom will you find cold remoteness in Texas, whether in a dizzying downtown or on the remotest ranch road. People seem free to open up in the Lone Star State, even the newcomers...or one might say, *especially* the newcomers. The Texas spirit is catching.

A.C. Greene
Dallas

Barbecued steaks and ribs ZIGY KALUZNY

A quarter horse and her foal   D.K. LANGFORD/NATURAL SELECTION

The bigness of Texas is in the land itself. Everywhere the earth is level, wide, and open, stretching away and away, under the vast panoply of the sky. Visitors may very well find it tedious, as one apparently featureless expanse dissolves into the next one. But, to a Texan, the immensity signifies freedom, the seeming emptiness is room for action, space for movement and growth.

Green Peyton,
The Face of Texas

Trailing cows near Falfurrias   ZIGY KALUZNY

Guadalupe Mountains rise behind white sand dunes in Guadalupe Mountains National Park   DAVID MUENCH

Mist at sunrise along San Antonio Bay   ELEANOR BROWN

“ *Texas has plains and mountains, sweeping beaches and deep forests, great seaports and teeming inland markets, crowded areas and vast open spaces, spots as comfortably civilized as Manhattan's Park Avenue, and spots as barrenly wild as Patagonia.* ”

The WPA Guide to Texas

El Capitan in the Guadalupe Mountains National Park   DAVID MUENCH

Seashells along the coast of Brazos Island   DAVID MUENCH

Bald cypress along Caddo Lake   DAVID MUENCH

The silhouette of a doe at sunset ENTHEOS

Lights on the Houston interstate   FRANK WHITNEY/THE IMAGE BANK

A blooming claret cup cactus at Big Bend National Park   TOM ALGIRE

Feeding cattle in the rain   RICHARD HAMILTON SMITH

> **"** *Stamina, individualism, "go-ahead" initiative, pride in everything Texan—these were and still are, in varying degrees, among the ingredients of the Texas spirit.* **"**

William Ransom Hogan,
The Texas Republic

Collecting seashells on Padre Island   LARRY MAYER

Off-shore drilling   BOB KELLER

A big Texas snowman   ROBERTA BARNES

Bike racing at the Fort Worth Stockyards   BEEBOWER BROS./PHOTOGRAPHIC RESOURCES

Crawling from Airman's Cave   LAURENCE PARENT

A horse roundup   MATT BRADLEY

A cowboy's quick lunch at Fort Davis   MATT BRADLEY

A solitary ranch   MATT BRADLEY

Sunset on the Chisos Mountains in Big Bend National Park   LAURENCE PARENT

For all its enormous range of space, climate, and physical appearance . . . Texas has a tight cohesiveness perhaps stronger than any other section of America. Rich, poor, Panhandle, Gulf, city, country, Texas is the . . . passionate possession of all Texans.

John Steinbeck,
Travels with Charley

Bigtooth maple leaves in water LAURENCE PARENT

Stalactites in the Caverns of Sonora LAURENCE PARENT

Sunrise over Austin   AMY KWALWASSER

" Texas with her superior natural advantages must become a point of attraction, and the policy of establishing with her the earliest relations of friendship and commerce will not escape the eye of statesmen. "

Sam Houston,
Sam Houston's Texas

Emory Peak in Big Bend National Park   DAVID MUENCH

Indian blanket flowers bloom on the Llano Uplift   DAVID MUENCH

White-tailed deer   ENTHEOS

" *Deer go with mornings. Sleepy and unfocused, I went into the woods for breakfast fuel and stood out of the still big wind in a sheltered place by a heap of fallen post oak, unwilling to rive the silence with my ax. She came picking her way along a fence line at right angles to me. Half catching my scent, she flicked up her tail and went away soundlessly and without desperate speed; then another came the same route, snuffed the whirlpooling scent full, coughed, and tore off across a field with a big fawn behind her.* "

John Graves,
Goodbye to a River

Prairie dogs   ENTHEOS

A fiery sunset on the Rio Grande CARL KURTZ

" *Texas is a state of mind. Texas is an obsession. Above all, Texas is a nation in every sense of the word.* *"*

John Steinbeck,
Travels with Charley

37

Primrose, paintbrush, and bluebonnet blooming in the Hill Country DAVID MUENCH

Oak Creek Canyon in Big Bend National Park   SCOTT T. SMITH

Lighthouse Rock in Palo Duro Canyon State Park   DAVID MUENCH

Alligator at Anahuac National Wildlife Refuge   ELEANOR BROWN

Blacktail jackrabbit   STEVEN M. ALDEN

Tricolored heron ELEANOR BROWN

Whitetail buck   STEVEN M. ALDEN

A play at Alamo Village in Brackettville   RICHARD STOCKTON/PHOTOGRAPHIC RESOURCES

" March 3. We have given over all hopes of receiving assistance from Goliad or Refugio. Colonel Travis harangued the garrison, and concluded by exhorting them, in case the enemy should carry the fort, to fight to the last gasp, and render their victory even more serious to them than to us. This was followed by three cheers.

March 5. Pop, pop, pop! Bom, bom, bom! throughout the day. No time for memorandums now. Go ahead! Liberty and independence forever! "

Davy Crockett,
The Autobiography of David Crockett

The Alamo in San Antonio   DAVID MUENCH

A cowboy's sunrise   TEXAS DEPT. OF COMMERCE

> *Out here it's impossible to be lonely.*
> *The land walking beside you is your oldest friend,*
> *pleasantly silent, like already you've told the best stories*
> *and each of you knows how much the other made up.*

Naomi Shihab Nye,
"At the Seven-Mile Ranch, Comstock, Texas"
Hugging the Jukebox

Autumn in Guadalupe Mountains National Park   RICHARD REYNOLDS/TEXAS DEPT. OF COMMERCE

Lava rocks in Big Bend National Park   TOM ALGIRE

Sunset over Daingerfield State Park   DAVID MUENCH

All the beauty of the landscape now was in the harmony of the valley rolling fluently away to the wood's edge. It was an inland country, with the forlorn look of all unloved things; winter in this part of the south is a moribund coma, not the northern death sleep with the sure promise of resurrection. But in my south, my loved and never-forgotten country, after her long sickness, with only a slight stirring, an opening of the eyes between one breath and the next, between night and day, the earth revives and bursts into the plenty of spring with fruit and flowers together, spring and summer at once under the hot shimmering blue sky.

Katherine Anne Porter,
"Holiday"
The Collected Stories of
Katherine Anne Porter

A bullfrog at Audubon Sanctuary Pond   ELEANOR BROWN

Armadillo   WYMAN P. MEINZER

50

Yucca and buckwheat DAVID MUENCH

Sweet pea   ENTHEOS

West of the Brazos, the land unfolded even farther to the blue sky. Now the horizon wasn't ten or fifteen miles away, it was thirty or forty. On telephone wires sat scissor-tailed flycatchers, their oddly long tails hanging under them like stilts. Roadside wildflowers—bluebonnets, purple winecups, evening primroses, and more—were abundant as crops, and where wide reaches of bluebonnets . . . covered the slopes, their scent filled the highway. To all the land was an intense clarity as if the little things gave off light.

William Least Heat Moon,
Blue Highways

Pink evening primrose   RON SANFORD

Whitetail doe and fawn in Brazos Bend State Park   ELEANOR BROWN

Least bittern chicks   ENTHEOS

Wildflowers and mesquite trees   DAVID MUENCH

Dallas at dusk   RICHARD REYNOLDS/TEXAS DEPT. OF COMMERCE

> *If we built tall enough, and we have the technological capability, we could double the world's population and still fit every single one of us into the state o' Texas. Comfortably, I might add.*

Tom Robbins,
Jitterbug Perfume

The Rio Grande flowing through Colorado Canyon   DAVID MUENCH

San Jacinto Monument   TEXAS DEPT. OF COMMERCE

Off-shore oil rig near Galveston   TONY SCHANUEL/PHOTOGRAPHIC RESOURCES

Brownsville Charro Days   TEXAS DEPT. OF COMMERCE

Nor is it a habit of Texans to look back. We have a tradition of looking forward and not looking back to see where we have been or who is following us. There is time enough for that when we are gone.

Lyndon B. Johnson,
The Lyndon Johnson Story

Sand sculpture on South Padre Island   RICHARD REYNOLDS/TEXAS DEPT. OF COMMERCE

President George Bush   ROBERTA BARNES

Vaqueros and longhorns   D.K. LANGFORD/NATURAL SELECTION

"   *The cowpuncher was a totally different class from these other fellows on the frontier. We was the salt of the earth, any way in our own estimation, and we had the pride that went with it.* "

Teddy Blue,
We Pointed Them North

Tubers on the Guadalupe River   RANDALL K. ROBERTS

Whitetail buck at sunset   STEVEN M. ALDEN

Dawn in the Big Bend National Park   MATT BRADLEY

Yucca   MATT BRADLEY

Texas thunderstorm   D.K. LANGFORD/NATURAL SELECTION

"No man with gumption would have thought of leaving Texas in the heraldic past, unless he were at gunpoint. There was too much excitement. Hell, a continent had to be explored, a wilderness subdued. . . . Longhorns had to be driven to market, railroads brought in, and oil rigs set in motion."

Bill Porterfield,
A Loose Herd of Texans

Cardinal   ELEANOR BROWN

" *It was an ageless land where the past was still a living thing and old voices still whispered, where the freshness of the pioneer time had not yet all faded, where a few of the old dreams were not yet dark with tarnish.* "

Elmer Kelton,
The Time It Never Rained

Bald cypress knees rising from Village Creek in Big Thicket National Preserve LAURENCE PARENT

Wild turkey STEVEN M. ALDEN

Green tree frog on pitcher plant   JESS ALFORD

Grouse under a stormy sky   ENTHEOS

“ *De vedder out here I do not like. De rain vas all vind, and de vind vas all sand.* ”

German settler talking about Amarillo,
Inside U.S.A.

Agave spike in the Big Bend National Park   DAVID MUENCH

White ibis in Brazos Bend State Park   ELEANOR BROWN

Herons and egrets   ENTHEOS

" *The bobwhites' cheerio to morning . . . the sandhill cranes fluting their long, long cries on a winter evening . . . the coyotes serenading from every side after dark . . . the green on the mesquites in early spring so tender that it emanated into the sky . . . the stillness of day and night broken by windmills lifting rods that lifted water . . . the locusts in the mulberry tree . . . the rhythm of a saddle's squeak in the night: these the land gave me.* "

J. Frank Dobie,
Some Part of Myself

Oil derrick under a red sun   D.K. LANGFORD/NATURAL SELECTION

Oil pumpjack   D.K. LANGFORD/NATURAL SELECTION

Herding at sunset   RICHARD REYNOLDS/TEXAS DEPT. OF COMMERCE

66 *The frontier experience gave Texans an identity, a feeling of folkhood beyond the reach of Ohioans or Oregonians. The frontier people did not so much "settle" Texas as conquer it. The true Texans—those descended in some way from the nineteenth-century people-making process—understand this. . . .* 99

T.R. Fehrenbach,
Seven Keys to Texas

Longhorn steer   D.K. LANGFORD/NATURAL SELECTION

Rodeo   MICHAEL MURPHY/TEXAS DEPT. OF COMMERCE

Cutting a cow   RICHARD HAMILTON SMITH

Monahans Sandhills State Park   DAVID MUENCH

Texas football game   D.K. LANGFORD/NATURAL SELECTION

" . . . certain fundamental facts must be remembered if you're searching for the true Texas character. . . . Nothing in life was bigger than Friday football, and when lights made it possible to play at night, even more people could attend and the field became a kind of cathedral under the stars. Now it was Friday Night Football, as grand an invention as man has made, with the entire community meeting for spiritual warmth. "

James Michener,
Texas

Cheerleaders at the University of Texas   ZIGY KALUZNY

Muskrat and wood duck   ENTHEOS

" . . . most of Texas beyond the pine woods is a country of rolling hills, broad prairies, rising limestone plateaus, and almost treeless plains, a land of vast horizons, a land where the natural tendency of man and animals is to be volatile and free. "

T.R. Fehrenbach,
Seven Keys to Texas

Prickly pear beneath Castolon Peak in Big Bend National Park   LAURENCE PARENT

Sea beans   ELEANOR BROWN

Golden eagle   D.K. LANGFORD/NATURAL SELECTION

A bass fisherman   WYMAN P. MEINZER JR.

Wind surfing at Corpus Christi   RICHARD REYNOLDS/TEXAS DEPT. OF COMMERCE

Girl and puppy at Brazos Bend State Park   WILLIAM D. ADAMS

Big Sandy Creek Unit in the Big Thicket Natural Preserve   DAVID MUENCH

> *Texas is the place where you need a mousetrap to catch mosquitoes, where a man is so hardboiled that he sleeps in sandpaper sheets . . . where Davy Crockett fanned himself with a hurricane . . . where houseflies carry dog tags for identification, and where that legendary creature Pecos Bill, the Texas equivalent of Paul Bunyan, could rope a streak of lightning.*

John Gunther,
Inside U.S.A.

Reflections in Oak Creek, Big Bend National Park   LAURENCE PARENT

Pecans   FRANK MOSTER

Cabbage patch   DAVID MUENCH

South Prong in the Caprock Canyons State Park   FRANK MOSTER

❝ *A Texas editor puts it in this epigrammatic way: "If you tipped the State up and dropped it north like a tossed pancake, it would knock down the skyscrapers of St. Paul; and east, El Paso would drop into the Atlantic; and south, the State would blot out most of Mexico. Of course Texas is big; children in school learn that it is big."* ❞

Nevin O. Winter,
Texas the Marvellous

Rio Grande at dusk   DAVID MUENCH

Road to the Guadalupe Mountains   WILLIAM D. ADAMS

Rafting the Guadalupe River   RICHARD REYNOLDS/TEXAS DEPT. OF COMMERCE

Horned lizard   ENTHEOS

Remnant live oaks at the Padre Island National Seashore   MATT BRADLEY

" *Why did men come to that once forbidding land? Well, they were restless, of course, and had to be moving on. But there was more than that. There was a dream—a dream of a place where a free man could build for himself, and raise his children to a better life—a dream of a continent to be conquered, a world to be won, a nation to be made.* **"**

Lyndon Baines Johnson,
State of the Union message, 1965

Cowboys on the South Double Diamond Ranch   TEXAS DEPT. OF COMMERCE

Branding irons   RICHARD HAMILTON SMITH

Turk's head cactus   LAURENCE PARENT

Firewheel bloom   ENTHEOS

Padre Island National Seashore   DAVID MUENCH

Baby burrowing owls   D. ROBERT FRANZ

Greater roadrunner   JOHN SHAW

A pet armadillo   WILLIAM D. ADAMS

Moon setting over a mesquite tree   FRANK MOSTER

“ *I never see these patches of sage grass without thinking of the vast extent of those grass-covered prairie plains. I think of them fenceless and abounding in wild life. On a gusty day the eye might trace sudden currents of air for miles, as they swept over gentle slopes, bending the tall grass, wave succeeding wave as on an ocean, driven along under the impulsion of the wind. . . .* **”**

Roy Bedichek,
Adventures with a Texas Naturalist

Pictograph masks at Hueco Tanks State Park   DAVID MUENCH

Tornado weather at sunset   RON SANFORD

" North Texas weather guarantees adventure. Some say we don't really have seasons here, we have erratically spaced endurance tests. Others say nature here's a prankster with a bias for the vicious—or the thrilling— depending on the amount of porcelain in your crop. "

James Hoggard,
Riding the Wind

Egrets along a coastal salt marsh near Freeport   LAURENCE PARENT

Bottomland fog near Argyle   FRANK MOSTER

❝ *I like the story, doubtless antique, that I heard near San Antonio. A child asks a stranger where he comes from, whereupon his father rebukes him gently, 'Never do that son. If a man's from Texas, he'll tell you. If he's not, why embarrass him by asking?'* **❞**

John Gunther,
Inside U.S.A.

Washington County Fair in Brenham   WILLIAM D. ADAMS

Loads of cotton   WILLIAM D. ADAMS

Pummel Peak behind snowy prickly pear in the Big Bend National Park   TOM ALGIRE

 " The region is not much like Europe, dominated by men back to a time before men's records begin. . . . It is not even like the Atlantic South, where . . . along the shore of a tidal river you can kick up English colonists' brickbats and winebottle shards from the 1600's. It is like Texas, where the civilized layers are shallow, but the traces and shades of people who have been here—as well as many who have not—matter so much that there is small chance of understanding the land without taking them a little into account. "

John Graves,
Hard Scrabble

Prickly pear cactus in bloom   TOM ALGIRE

I must say as to what I have seen of Texas it is the garden spot of the world. The best land and the best prospects for health I ever saw, and I do believe it is a fortune to any man to come here. There is a world of country here to settle.

Davy Crockett

113

Wildflowers at Enchanted Rock   DAVID MUENCH

Port of Corpus Christi   DAVID MUENCH

Padre Island National Seashore   MATT BRADLEY

United States and Texas flags   WILLIAM D. ADAMS

they made it possible

Texas on My Mind would have been impossible to produce without the keen eyes and technical skills of more than forty professional photographers. These men and women succeeded in a difficult task—capturing the many moods and faces of Texas.

From the Panhandle to the Gulf Coast, from the eastern pine woods to the lonely Big Bend, Texas contains an astonishing array of beautiful images, but transforming these images onto film requires more than just a camera. It takes an eye for composition, technical expertise, the willingness to work in all weather, and, perhaps most important, the extra effort and patience that often separates an extraordinary photograph from a mere snapshot.

The photographers for *Texas on My Mind* provided this effort. They hiked, climbed, paddled, crawled, and even flew to get the best possible images.

To all the excellent photographers who contributed to *Texas on My Mind*, thank you.

Michael S. Sample and Bill Schneider
Publishers, Falcon Publishing

A river canyon   MATT BRADLEY

Photographers in *Texas on my Mind*

William D. Adams	Zigy Kaluzny	Michael Murphy	Richard Stockton
Steven M. Alden	Bob Keller	Laurence Parent	Frank Whitney
Jess Alford	Carl Kurtz	Richard Reynolds	And these photo agencies:
Tom Algire	Amy Kwalwasser	Randall K. Roberts	Entheos
Roberta Barnes	D.K. Langford	Ron Sanford	Natural Selection
Beebower Bros.	Larry Mayer	Tony Schanuel	Photographic Resources
Matt Bradley	Wyman P. Meinzer Jr.	John Shaw	The Image Bank
Eleanor Brown	Frank Moster	R. Hamilton Smith	Tourism Division/Texas
D. Robert Franz	David Muench	Scott T. Smith	Department of Commerce

acknowledgments

The publishers gratefully acknowledge the following sources:

Page 8 from *The Face of Texas* by Green Peyton. Copyright © 1961 by Green Peyton. Published by Bonanza Books, a division of Random House.

Page 12 from *The WPA Guide to Texas.* Reprinted by permission of Texas Monthly Press.

Page 20 from *The Texas Republic: A Social and Economic History* by William Ranson Hogan. Copyright © 1946 by the Univerity of Oklahoma Press.

Pages 26 and 36 from *Travels with Charley* by John Steinbeck. Copyright © 1961, 1962 by The Curtis Publishing Co., Inc. Reprinted by permission of Viking Penguin, a division of Penguin Books USA, Inc.

Page 32 from *Goodbye to a River* by John Graves. Copyright © 1960 by John Graves. Reprinted by permission of Alfred A. Knopf, Inc.

Page 44 from *The Autobiography of David Crockett* by David Crockett. Copyright © 1923 by Charles Scribner's Sons; copyright renewed. Reprinted by permission of Charles Scribner's Sons, an imprint of Macmillan Publishing Company.

Page 46 from "At the Seven-mile Ranch, Comstock, Texas," by Naomi Shihab Nye. *Hugging the Jukebox.* Copyright © 1987 by Breitenbush Books. Reprinted by permission of the author.

Page 50 from "Holiday," by Katherine Anne Porter. Copyright © 1960 by Katherine Anne Porter and renewed 1988 by Isabel Bayley. From *The Collected Stories of Katherine Anne Porter.* Reprinted by permission of Harcourt Brace Jovanovich, Inc.

Page 52 from *Blue Highways* by William Least Heat Moon. Copyright © 1982 by William Least Heat Moon. Reprinted by permission of Little, Brown and Company.

Page 56 from *Jitterbug Perfume* by Tom Robbins. Copyright © 1984 by Tibetan Peach Pie, Inc. Published by Bantam Books, a division of Bantam Doubleday Dell Publishing Group, Inc.

Page 62 from *We Pointed Them North* by E.C. Abbott ("Teddy Blue") and Helena Huntington Smith. Copyright © 1954 by the University of Oklahoma Press.

Page 67 from *A Loose Herd of Texans* by Bill Porterfield. Copyright © 1978 by Bill Porterfield. Reprinted by permission of Texas A&M University Press.

Page 68 from *The Time It Never Rained* by Elmer Kelton. Copyright © 1973 by Elmer Kelton. Reprinted by permission of Doubleday, a division of Bantam Doubleday Dell Publishing Group, Inc.

Pages 72, 90, and 109 from *Inside U.S.A.* by John Gunther. Copyright © 1951 by John Gunther. Reprinted by permission of Harper & Row, Publishers, Inc.

Page 75 from *Some Part of Myself* by J. Frank Dobie. Copyright © 1967 by Bertha Dobie. Reprinted by permission of Little, Brown and Company.

Pages 77 and 84 from *Seven Keys to Texas* by T.R. Fehrenbach. Copyright © 1983 by Texas Western Press of the University of Texas at El Paso.

Page 82 from *Texas* by James A. Michener. Copyright © 1985 by James A. Michener. Reprinted by permission of Ballantine Books.

Page 105 from *Adventures with a Texas Naturalist* by Roy Bedichek. Copyright © 1961 by Lillian G. Bedichek; copyright renewed 1989. Reprinted by permisson of the University of Texas Press.

Page 107 from "Riding the Wind," *Southwest Review,* Summer 1982. Reprinted by permission of the author, James Hoggard.

Page 111 from *Hard Scrabble* by John Graves. Copyright © 1974 by John Graves. Reprinted by permission of Alfred A. Knopf, Inc.

Mockingbird on cholla catcus   WYMAN P. MEINZER, JR.

About A.C. Greene

Texas author A.C. Greene wrote the introduction to *Texas on my Mind*. A Texas native, Greene is widely considered one of the state's most influential historians. His own writings include *A Personal Country* and a dozen other books about life in Texas, and he has contributed to numerous anthologies and magazines. Greene's column, "Texas Sketches," appears in several Texas newspapers. Greene also has worked in television, radio, film, and drama, and he is Resident Professor of Texas Studies and Coordinating Director of the Center for Texas Studies at the University of North Texas. He lives in Dallas.

Sunrise over Galveston Bay   MICHAEL MURPHY/TEXAS DEPT. OF COMMERCE